MAY CHINN

THE BEST MEDICINE

MAY CHINN

THE BEST MEDICINE

BY ELLEN R. BUTTS & JOYCE R. SCHWARTZ

ILLUSTRATED BY JANET HAMLIN

BOOKS FOR YOUNG READERS
Scientific American

W. H. FREEMAN AND COMPANY ◆ NEW YORK

Book design by Debora Smith

Scientific American Books for Young Readers is an imprint of
W. H. Freeman and Company, 41 Madison Avenue
New York, New York, 10010

Library of Congress Cataloging-in-Publication Data

Butts, Ellen

May Chinn: the best medicine / by Ellen Butts and Joyce Schwartz;

illustrated by Janet Hamlin.

p. cm.

Includes index

ISBN 0-7167-6589-6 (hbk.).—ISBN 0-7167-6590-x (pbk.)

1. Chinn, May Edward, 1896-1980—Juvenile literature. 2. Public health personnel—New York (N.Y.)—Biography—Juvenile literature. 4. Women physicians—New York (N.Y.)—Biography—Juvenile literature. [1. Chinn, May Edward, 1896-1980. 2. Physicians. 3. Women—Biography.] I. Schwartz, Joyce. II. Hamlin, Janet, ill. III. Title.

RA424.5.C565B88 1995

610'.92—dc20

[B]   94-35395

CIP

AC

Printed in the United States of America

10 9 8 7 6 5 4 3 2 1

To the memory of my mother, Norma Rubinstein, who imbued me
with her belief that if it could be done, I could do it—ERB

In memory of my grandmother, Elsie Gelpi, whose courage
and goodness inspired all who knew her—JRS

CONTENTS

CHAPTER 1

The Land of Opportunity

Three-year-old May Chinn gazed from her apartment window into the dark alley below. New York City seemed a long way from the quiet Massachusetts town where she was born.

The Chinns' cold and gloomy one-room apartment was so small that they had to cover the bathtub with boards when they needed a table. The only source of heat was a stove that burned coal or wood—when there was enough money to buy fuel. There was no hot water, and they had to walk through another apartment to reach the bathroom. Conditions were terrible, but the Chinns had little choice.

In the spring of 1899 there were three million people in New York City. Crowded apartment buildings like the Chinns' lined many city blocks, and the daily lives of people packed into small spaces spilled out onto the streets. Many poor, uneducated immigrants had fled the ghettoes and slums of Ireland, Germany, Italy and Russia to find opportunity in the United States. The clatter of children playing, the cries of street vendors, and the babble of foreign languages created a constant commotion.

Not all the people who came to New York City that spring were from foreign countries. May's father had decided that New York City

was the best place for him to find a good job. Like the European immigrants, William Chinn, an African American, had hoped to find a better life. But he had to compete with many others for work, and many business owners discriminated against African Americans—they refused to hire black people, for no other reason than the color of their skin.

May Edward Chinn was born on April 15, 1896. Though she always called herself a "Negro," May was actually part African American, part Native American, and part Caucasian.

Lulu Ann Chinn, May's mother, was born in 1876 on a reservation near Norfolk, Virginia, the daughter of a Chickahominy Indian mother and an African-American father. She was poor and uneducated and at fifteen went to work as a maid for a Virginia family. When her employers moved to Great Barrington, Massachusetts, Lulu went along. She soon met and married the handsome, dapper, and much older William Chinn.

William had been born a slave on a plantation in Virginia, probably the son of one of the plantation's white owners and an African-American slave woman. William was only eleven years old when he escaped from the plantation and fled to Great Barrington, where he worked for several years at a variety of unskilled jobs. William was very light skinned, and he dressed like an English gentleman. In his three-piece suit and derby hat, he could have passed for an English gentleman. But he never denied his African-American heritage, despite the prejudice he faced.

May Edward Chinn was born on April 15, 1896. Her almond-shaped eyes, fair skin, and high cheekbones showed her mixed heritage. Many times throughout May's long life people would assume she was Chinese because of her looks and her name, which sounded like the common Chinese name Chin.

William struggled to find a job, but each day ended in frustration until, in despair and anger, he began to drink. Often when William had had too much to drink, he would yell and curse at Lulu.

Although jobs for African-American men were scarce, the women could usually find employment cleaning other people's houses, so Lulu became a maid. Despite the long hours she worked, her meager earnings were barely enough to pay for food and rent.

The Chinns had arrived in New York City full of high hopes. But now their dreams seemed to be collapsing around them. Life was difficult and dreary, filled with hard work and poverty. Would it always be the same? Was there any escape?

CHAPTER 2

Rags and Riches

Even if Lulu had to work the rest of her life as a servant, she wanted to make sure that May would have something better. Lulu knew that a good education was the key, and she worked extra hard so that there would be money for May's schooling.

By the time May was five, Lulu had scraped together enough money to send her to a boarding school for African-American children in a peaceful New Jersey town. There May could escape the noise and poverty of her New York neighborhood and the misery created by her father's drinking. She could begin the long journey out of poverty.

But soon after she started school, May got a serious infection called osteomyelitis in her jawbone. Today such infections can be cured with antibiotics, but in 1901 these bacteria-fighting medicines were unknown. The only treatment available at that time was surgery. May had nine different operations and had to wear a large bandage around her head. The pain was so terrible that she often had to eat her meals and study her lessons in bed. It soon became clear that she would have to go home.

May's illness left a small dent in the right side of her jaw. As an adult she had plastic surgery to remove the scar, but she always remembered feeling ugly because of it. When May was much older, she looked back on a photo of herself as a teenager. "You'll notice you can only see the left side of my face," she explained. "On the right side I had this depressed area from the childhood illness. This had made me terribly shy."

While May was at boarding school, William moved to another part of New York City hoping, in vain, to find steady employment. Fortunately, Lulu found work as a live-in cook at Tiffany Hall, the country estate of Charles Lewis Tiffany. When May was sent home from boarding school, she joined her mother at the estate in a wealthy area north of New York City. Her most wonderful dreams could not have prepared her for what lay ahead.

Charles Tiffany, almost ninety at the time, was one of the wealthiest men in New York. He had founded Tiffany & Company, a fashionable store known for its elegant jewelry and silver. His oldest son, Louis Comfort Tiffany, was world famous for his unique stained-glass lamps and windows. Louis had seven children who loved to visit their grandfather's summer home.

It was a joyous time for May. How far she and Lulu had come from their dreary one-room apartment! The upper-class Tiffanys didn't care what color her skin was—they treated May like a member of the family. Being part of a large family was a new experience for May, an only child. She and the Tiffany children spent hours playing

all over the huge estate. They ate together, took French and German lessons together and—best of all—attended plays and concerts together in New York City. On those magical trips, May discovered what would become a life-long love—music.

Sadly, May's happy time at Tiffany Hall lasted less than a year. In early 1902, Charles Tiffany died and Lulu was no longer needed. She and May rejoined William in New York City and once again, poverty seemed inescapable.

But May still had music. Lulu arranged for her to take piano lessons and bought an old, broken-down piano, all she could afford. May's greatest pleasures were playing and singing, and she often performed in recitals. Her usual shyness disappeared in front of an audience.

Lulu still firmly believed in the importance of a good education, and she moved the family often to take advantage of neighborhoods with good schools. Many years later May remembered, "This was very important to my mother. She would wait to see a neighborhood

opening up and she would be among the first Negroes to move in before the whites all moved away...." As long as a school still had white children in it, the school system paid more attention to it.

The Chinns left Manhattan for the Bronx, so May could enroll in Morris High School, one of the finest schools in the city. They moved to an apartment near a piano factory. Although William and Lulu still earned very little money, living close to the factory must have inspired them. On May's sixteenth birthday they surprised her with a piano so new the varnish wasn't even dry. She had to wait three days before she could play it!

At last it seemed that Lulu's plans would become a reality. The family was together and May was attending a good school. The new piano sang with a voice of hope.

CHAPTER 3

A Woman's Place

Although Lulu desperately wanted a good education for her daughter, William had other ideas about May's future. At age sixteen, May attracted the attention of a widowed businessman who lived across the street. Dressed in his best clothes, he visited the Chinns and asked permission to marry "little May."

Even though Lulu had married William when she was sixteen and he was forty, she was appalled at the idea of her daughter marrying so young. William disagreed. He felt that marriage to a successful businessman was the best opportunity for a young woman. When May refused the widower's offer, her father was so furious he wouldn't speak to her. Since May never married, he stayed angry for years.

Now that he had a steady job as a night porter at a respectable Manhattan store, William took care to wear only the best clothes, and although he still drank heavily, his behavior was formal and dignified. Even though May was a responsible teenager, William frequently lectured her about the dangers of smoking, chewing gum and—especially—staying single. He even began to consider May's musical interests improper. Much to his disgust, Lulu permitted May to sing and act in musical productions. Worse yet, May sometimes marched in suffragette parades in support of women's voting rights.

Perhaps the poverty and constant arguing were too much for May, or maybe a failed romance or a bad grade upset her. But without warning, she dropped out of eleventh grade. Lulu was heartbroken. May went to work in a factory, where she spent long, dull days tying ribbons in calendars. In her spare time she gave piano lessons to kindergarten children.

One of May's friends was attending Columbia University's Teachers College. About a year after May had dropped out of school, the

friend convinced her to take the Teachers College entrance exam, just to see how she would do. May's score was so high she was accepted as a full-time college student, even though she hadn't graduated high school!

Lulu's dream had come true. But William thought little of his daughter's accomplishment. She had passed the entrance exam, but where would she find the money for tuition? Even if he could afford it, William wouldn't pay for a college education he felt was unnecessary. He still believed that a woman should be content with marriage and a family.

Once again, Lulu took charge. For years, she had been secretly putting aside part of the money she earned scrubbing floors and cooking for wealthy people. She kept the money tied up in a cloth, which she wore to bed every night to guard its precious contents. Now she triumphantly produced her savings: four hundred dollars, enough for two years of tuition. May was going to college!

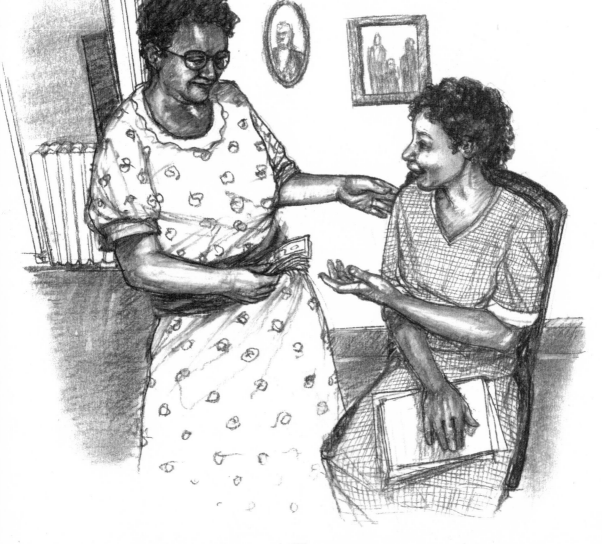

CHAPTER 4

Turning Point

When May entered Columbia University's Teachers College in 1917, she was one of 2,300 students from all over the United States and the world. The imposing stone buildings of the college would be her second home for the next four years.

May planned to study music. With a college degree, she could earn a living teaching piano and performing at concerts. But one of her first music classes turned into an encounter with discrimination. May was the only woman and the only African American in the class—the other eleven students were white and male. She was shy and self-conscious, and to make matters worse, the professor either ignored or ridiculed her. He believed that African Americans appreciated only jazz and blues and could never understand classical music.

Even though May earned a "B" in the course, when she discovered that she'd have to take five more classes with the same professor, she decided her plans to study music were impossible. At that time, laws against discrimination did not exist. There was nothing she could do about the professor's prejudice, no way to fight back.

Merely to fulfill her credit requirements, May had signed up for a hygiene course taught by a biologist named Jean Broadhurst. As a final project, May wrote a paper called "Sewage Disposal." A few days

later Dr. Broadhurst asked to see her. "I never expected such an interesting paper from a person whose major is music," Dr. Broadhurst said. After they chatted for a while, Dr. Broadhurst ended their meeting by saying, "If by chance you change your major, consider science, and contact me." She told May that science could offer her a bright future.

May knew she had to choose between music and science. Teachers in the music department warned her that because she was African-American, she would have to go to Europe to get experience as a performer and refine her talent. If she stayed in the United States, she could become nothing more than a nightclub singer. May considered herself a serious musician and did not look forward to performing in nightclubs for the rest of her life.

On the other hand, Dr. Broadhurst pointed out that—even though there were some prejudiced people in every field—in science, a person's ability and hard work mattered a lot more than the color of her skin. Dr. Broadhurst was certain that May could get a job doing research and offered to help her get enough work to finance her tuition.

What should she do? Stay with music, her first love, and face an uncertain future? Or choose an entirely different career, one that would provide her with a good job? Practical considerations won, and what had started out as a crisis became the turning point in May's life. At the beginning of her second year May changed her major to science.

The remaining three years were hectic but rewarding. Dr. Broadhurst was like a second mother, advising May and arranging for her to work in the college's science department and at outside laboratories. May continued taking singing lessons in Columbia's music department, accompanying other students on the piano as payment.

During her senior year, May attended classes at night and worked as a clinical pathologist during the day. Clinical pathologists learn about the causes of disease by studying tissue samples removed from patients. Each organ in the body, like the liver, lungs, and brain, is composed of its own kind of tissue which, in turn, is composed of cells. Cells are so tiny they can be seen only under a microscope. Tiny as they are, they are the basic units of all living things, just as letters are the basic units of books.

One of May's most important jobs in the laboratory was to prepare tissue samples for study under a microscope. She had to cut slices of tissue thin enough for light to pass through. Then she attached the slices to small rectangular glass plates called slides. Finally, she had to stain the slides with special dyes to make the tissues and cells more visible under a microscope. After many hours of painstaking work

making slides, May studied them under her microscope to find out how the tissues had become diseased. Using her findings, doctors could then treat their patients effectively.

May's life ambition had been transformed. She was studying for a career she'd never even imagined! In the face of prejudice, May had made a sensible, practical decision and overcome yet another challenge.

CHAPTER 5

In the Middle of It All

Columbia University stands at the southern edge of a New York neighborhood called Harlem. In 1917, Lulu had moved the family to Harlem so that May could walk to college. In the early 1900s, Harlem was a fashionable neighborhood for white, upper-middle-class New Yorkers, including many politicians and wealthy businessmen. Luxurious brownstone houses lined the quiet streets, and several imposing mansions were scattered about. Along the wide avenues Harlem's residents could browse in a variety of shops and department stores. Many theaters, a music hall and an opera house provided them with every imaginable form of entertainment.

By 1911, a small number of African Americans had settled in central Harlem. Within three years, their population had expanded to 50,000. People of African heritage were pouring in from all over the United States and the Caribbean, eager to make a better life as part of an energetic and optimistic community. Almost every important African-American organization and institution had moved to Harlem, and it quickly became a cultural, intellectual and political center. Many brilliant leaders, such as W. E. B. Du Bois, leader of the civil rights movement and founder of the National Association for the Advancement of Colored People (NAACP) debated and wrote about the need for African-American political power and higher education. Marcus Garvey attracted tens of thousands to his Universal Negro Improvement Association by calling for African Americans to set up separate economic and social organizations and plan to return to Africa.

By the early 1920s, the jazz scene was at its height and Harlem became the heart of New York City's nightlife. It was the place to hear new music, dance new dances, and mingle with the trendsetters of the fashionable world. Every night thousands of well-dressed visitors, attracted to the blazing lights of Harlem, danced until dawn to the music of such soon-to-be legends as composers Duke Ellington, Eubie Blake, and Fats Waller and singers Ethel Waters and Bessie Smith.

A vibrant culture bloomed all around May. Along with the great musicians, many talented young writers migrated to Harlem. Novelists and poets such as Langston Hughes, James Weldon Johnson, and Zora Neale Hurston lived and worked, and shared the same goal—to write about everyday, working-class African Americans. Harlem became the setting for many of their creations. Langston Hughes wrote: "We younger Negro artists . . . now intend to express our individual dark-skinned selves without fear or shame. If white people are pleased, we are glad. If they are not, it doesn't matter. We know we are beautiful. And ugly too."

May, busy with school and work, had very little time to take in the wonders of Harlem. She did meet Langston Hughes and Zora Neale Hurston, and for a while dated an up-and-coming young writer named Rudolph Fisher. But perhaps her most exciting friendship was with a man named Paul Robeson.

Paul was an All-American college football player and a baseball, basketball, and track star. An excellent student, he graduated at the top of his college class. Then he earned a law degree from Columbia University while supporting himself by playing professional football

on the weekends. Although his intelligence and athletic abilities were outstanding, his greatest gift was his melodic and powerful baritone voice.

May often played and sang at recitals. One day, as she waited to perform, May heard a distinctive voice. Turning, she looked up at a very tall, handsome man. It was Paul Robeson. To her surprise, he asked if she would substitute for his accompanist, who was late.

Paul was already well-known in the New York City area, and May encouraged him to make music his career. Paul often practiced at her home, where May would accompany him on the piano. They began giving recitals together in small concert halls, churches, and private homes. Their physical appearance, as well as their music, must have been remarkable: May, five feet tall and plumpish next to Paul, over six feet tall and powerfully built.

For three or four years, whenever May had the time, she and Paul traveled throughout New York, New Jersey, and Connecticut, performing and sharing adventures. Even though they were just friends, Lulu always insisted they be home before morning.

Eventually, Paul and May spent less time together. As Paul became a world-famous actor and singer, May became immersed in her scientific studies. She would always play the piano for pleasure, but the career she was about to choose would demand all her attention.

CHAPTER 6

Career and Conflict

May's decision to study science instead of music had been courageous and practical. After graduating from college, though, she made a truly extraordinary choice. She decided to become a doctor. Only 65 out of 150,000 doctors in the United States at that time were African-American women. May remembered the "kindly nurses and doctors" who had cared for her when she had osteomyelitis as a child. And she knew that her community needed doctors.

Harlem's dramatic growth had started to show a less attractive side. Much of the area was terribly overcrowded. Work was hard to find, and crime and violence were all too common. With so many people crammed so close together, sickness seemed to be everywhere.

With Dr. Broadhurst's encouragement, May applied to Bellevue Medical College. As part of the application process, May had an interview with the assistant dean of the medical school, who knew that she had played piano for Paul Robeson. The dean was so interested in talking about Paul that he almost forgot to ask May about herself. After being admitted to Bellevue, May teased Paul, saying that she had gotten in because she knew him.

In the fall of 1922, May began a grueling four years of study and work. After attending classes all day and working in a pathology laboratory until late at night, she had to walk home past the enticing nightclubs of Harlem. Although her busy schedule once again left little time for having fun with friends, her hard work and long hours paid off. In 1926, May Chinn became the first African-American woman to graduate from Bellevue Medical College.

At age thirty, May had surpassed her mother's dreams. Not only had she graduated from college, but she had become a doctor when very few women could even imagine such an accomplishment. "I remember thinking that being a doctor was like waking up in a strange place and not knowing how I got there," she once said.

With medical school behind her, May was selected to be an intern at Harlem Hospital, the first African-American woman accepted there. The work was hard, the hours were long, and interns did not get paid. May had hoped to support her parents. Lulu had a heart condition, and May wished her mother did not have to spend nights cleaning office buildings. But for now, May had to continue living on her mother's earnings.

To make matters worse, May also continued to face discrimination. The male doctors at the hospital resented the presence of a woman intern and made May's life miserable. "They forgave and forgot their own mistakes," she lamented, "but they were often unkind and unforgetful of mine." As the only woman doctor on the staff, May had no one to turn to for sympathy. To escape the unfriendly stares and unkind words of the other doctors in the hospital, she began riding the ambulance on emergency calls, something no other woman had ever done.

When May first started making emergency calls, the ambulance drivers were so worried about her safety that they made sure she had a police escort when she visited Harlem's crowded tenements. Some of the poor people who lived there were so desperate that they might have stolen her coat if she took it off to care for a patient. As conditions grew more crowded and the neighborhood grew more violent, May was often called upon to treat stabbing or gunshot victims.

Racing to emergency calls may have been dangerous, but May preferred it to her regular duties. When she was in college and medical school, she had enjoyed the exuberance and creativity of Harlem's artists, writers, and musicians; now she was doing her best to aid its poorest residents. May's internship ended in 1928, but her service to the Harlem community was just beginning.

As May entered medical practice, she faced the problems that any new young doctor might have—a shortage of money and the need to build a reputation. But, as always, she was also forced to confront racial discrimination. Today, although racism unfortunately still exists,

there are laws against discrimination. In the 1920s and 1930s, however, New York City hospitals could legally refuse to let African-American physicians join their staffs or study in their programs and clinics. In order to have access to basic medical equipment, African-American doctors had to set up their own small hospitals.

May would not let discrimination prevent her from starting a medical practice. She opened an office on the ground floor of a brownstone on Edgecombe Avenue, one of Harlem's most fashionable streets. She and her parents lived on the second floor. The third floor served as an operating room for the Edgecombe Sanitarium, a small, simply equipped hospital located in the adjoining building. Because New York City law required hospitals to have a doctor present at all times, the seven African-American male doctors who owned the hospital rented space to the Chinn family in exchange for May's services as their night-duty physician.

Although some male doctors in Harlem were happy to take advantage of May's services for their late-night emergencies, others either ignored her existence or resented her for competing with them for patients. But the doctors from Edgecombe soon began sending their families to May, who treated them for free, as was the custom among doctors. Word spread, and more and more doctors—including some who had ignored her before—sent their wives and children to the new young woman doctor. May didn't make much money, sometimes less than fifty dollars a week, but her reputation was established and she began to feel accepted as a colleague by the other physicians in the neighborhood.

Gradually May developed what she called a "practice for rejects," offering her services to those who might not be able to get treatment anywhere else. She took care of the Handmaids of Mary (an order of African-American nuns), street people from Harlem, the wives of a group of Mohawk Indians who were doing construction work in Harlem, and women like her own mother, who were forced to clean houses for as little as twenty-five cents a day. May always preferred to practice family medicine and especially liked caring for women and children.

Many years before, May had made a choice simply to do what was practical. But her work now was so much more than that. May's life was becoming truly entwined with the lives of her patients and the community of Harlem.

CHAPTER 7

A Healing Hand

In the late 1920s, Harlem began to change from a haven for African-American artists and intellectuals to an overcrowded community struggling against poverty and crime.

Through her work, May witnessed the increasing misery of her patients' lives and did what she could to help. Conditions in the packed apartments were terrible: plumbing was inadequate, often there was no electricity, and several people might share the same bed. May also saw countless cases of food poisoning among her poorer patients, because many did not have adequate refrigeration to keep food fresh.

Along with poverty and overcrowding, drug addiction was also on the rise, bringing new danger to Harlem. May saw many addicts on the streets, including pregnant women. When a woman takes drugs during pregnancy, the drugs travel through the umbilical cord, just like food, to the baby, who may then be born addicted. May once had to care for a newborn whose mother had been an addict. As she listened to the infant's pitiful cries and watched its tiny body shake, May realized that drugs could destroy the neighborhood.

34

May's friends worried about her safety, particularly when she made late-night calls. One friend even bought her a gun and taught her how to use it. But May continued to make house calls, even at night. She was more concerned for her patients than she was for herself.

During the 1920s, many poor African Americans from the rural South migrated to New York, hoping to improve their lives. Just as William Chinn had discovered many years earlier, good jobs for men were scarce. The women spent their days looking for work or cleaning other people's houses, and left their children to take care of themselves. Often May would rush to the scene of an accident and find several young children in an apartment, all alone. "People who came from rural areas with strong morals soon lost them in this scramble to survive," May observed. "Some historians say that these periods of urban migration did more to destroy the Negro family than the several hundred years of slavery. I can believe this because of what I saw."

Because May and the other African-American doctors in Harlem still couldn't practice in most hospitals, they often had to operate in their patients' homes. They saw firsthand the terrible living conditions in the tenements. Although May had learned the latest medical techniques during her internship, she was forced to practice medicine as if they didn't exist.

May often helped Dr. Peter Marshal Murray, a well-known surgeon. They used a bed or an ironing board as their operating table, sterilizing their instruments on the coal stove. They had to bring their office lamps for light because their patients often had only kerosene lamps. Grandmothers and aunts took care of the patient after surgery and were, in May's opinion, "the best nurses in the world."

To better serve the community, May needed to understand the connection between her patients' unhealthy living conditions and their illnesses. Despite her heavy workload, she made time to return to

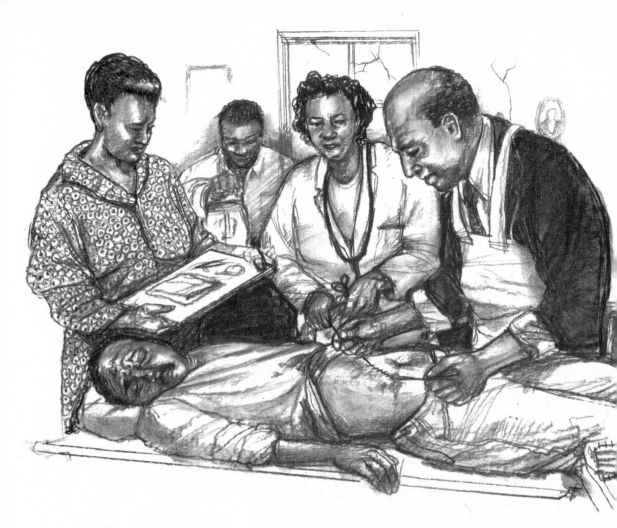

school. In 1933, Columbia University awarded her a master's degree in public health. For the next forty years, May worked for the New York City Department of Public Health, mainly examining and treating children in public day care centers. At the same time, she kept up her private practice.

May was particularly interested in treating women, and wanted to know more about their special health problems. Between 1928 and 1933, she studied with Dr. George Papanicolaou, who had made a breakthrough discovery in the detection of cervical cancer. The cervix is the opening to the uterus, the organ inside the mother's body where a baby develops. Sometimes the cells that line the cervix become cancerous. Dr. Papanicolaou discovered a painless new way to test the cervix for cancer. The "Pap" smear is a technique that is still used today and has saved the lives of thousands of women. May's work with Dr. Papanicolaou helped her to take better care of her female patients and extended her knowledge of clinical pathology.

Although May helped many people survive life in Harlem, there were some things beyond her control. In 1935, a major race riot took place in Harlem, started by the rumor that an African-American teenager had been beaten to death for stealing a ten-cent pocketknife from a department store. When the riot ended, the mayor of New York City asked a committee of black and white New Yorkers to study the causes of the riot. May was named to this committee, which recommended ways to improve the lives of Harlem's poor and deal with the explosive subject of racism.

Later, May worked on other committees that tackled the problems faced by African-American doctors in New York City. The efforts of May and her colleagues produced results: Harlem Hospital finally allowed African-American physicians to work and study in some of its clinics. By the time the United States entered World War II in December 1941, all of New York City's hospitals and clinics had opened their doors to qualified doctors of all backgrounds.

May's dedication to civil rights continued throughout her life. Her behavior was dignified and gentle, but she was always willing to protest injustice. Just as she had once marched in suffragette parades, she joined the 1963 march on Washington led by Dr. Martin Luther King, Jr., to call attention to the discrimination suffered by African Americans.

Between her busy work schedule and her dedication to important causes, May had little time for a private life. She was engaged several times, but never married. Although she never started a family of her own, May loved children and was godmother to nineteen of them, including the children of some of her former fiancés!

May's own parents were growing old, and her father became so ill that he needed surgery. May took care of him afterward, and during their long hours together they got to know and like each other again. Before he died in 1936, William forgave May for not marrying and even admitted that he was proud of her accomplishments.

Although her father was gone, May still had her mother's love and companionship. But six years later, Lulu died of a heart attack. Suddenly May had lost the one person who had been completely devoted to her, who had always believed in her and encouraged her to do her best. For the first time in her life, May was alone.

CHAPTER 8

Research and Recognition

With her small family gone now, May dug deeper than ever into her work. Her time with Dr. Papanicolaou had filled her with curiosity about cancer, and she strived to learn all she could.

Even today, many people don't know much about cancer, but just thinking about it can be very scary. Cancer is an out-of-control growth of cells. It can begin in many parts of the body, including the skin and blood. Some cancers grow very fast, while others spread very slowly. People with cancer often endure great pain.

When May was in medical school in the 1920s, very little was known about the disease. In her four years of classes, only one lecture about cancer was offered. Back then, there was no way to fight cancer, and the only treatment available was to inject a painkilling drug.

During the early years of her practice, May became increasingly concerned because many of her patients suffered from cancer. They were too poor or too frightened to go to the hospital, and it was usually too late to help them. Besides, all she could do was relieve some of the pain. No one could cure the disease. There were so many questions: Wasn't there some way to detect the disease before it was too late? Couldn't a patient be tested when symptoms first appeared, so early treatment could cure the cancer? Could it be stopped from spreading? Finding the answers became May's "fanatic preoccupation."

The basic step in diagnosing cancer is called a biopsy. When cells or tissues are suspected of being abnormal, they are removed from the patient and examined under a microscope. Although May had already spent several years working in a laboratory as a clinical pathologist, she now had to learn the special techniques used in biopsies. But that seemed impossible, because African Americans had not yet been allowed into the hospitals and clinics where biopsies were performed. Once again, discrimination stood in her way.

But once again, May refused to give up. As in the past, she had to be both persistent and clever to reach her goal. Sometimes, she heard of someone who needed a biopsy and would accompany that person to the clinic as his or her doctor. As a courtesy she was allowed to observe and ask questions. Or she would sneak into a hospital and friendly white doctors would secretly allow her to watch them conduct the procedure. One time ". . . I ran into an old college professor who told me that if I came to his office, he would show me how to do a biopsy. I was overjoyed."

Eventually, May began performing her own biopsies, sending tissue samples to Memorial Hospital because it was close to Harlem and she knew many physicians there. Soon May's reputation spread, and other African-American doctors sent her their patients' biopsies. She would then submit them to the hospital under her name. At last her hard work and devotion were being rewarded—she was helping to find cancers earlier, an important step toward her goal of preventing the disease.

But a further, unexpected reward was yet to come. In 1944, as she was about to leave on a hard-earned vacation, May received a telephone call from Dr. Elise Strang L'Espérance, a respected leader in the detection, diagnosis, and early treatment of cancer, especially in women. Dr. L'Espérance had founded three Strang Clinics that were

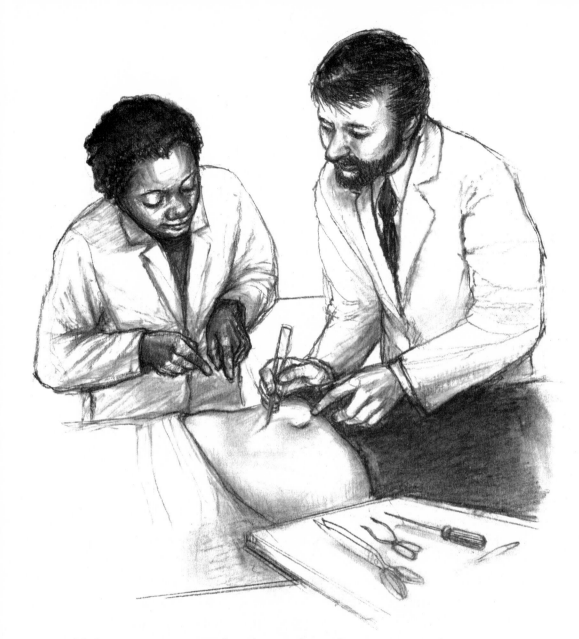

world famous as centers for the study and prevention of cancer—exactly the kind of research that was May's passion.

Elise knew about May's work and called to invite her for a job interview. May worried, "Does she know I am not Chinese as the name Chinn might imply, but was of African heritage?" Although Elise looked closely at May, she said nothing about race. Shortly afterward May was asked to work at the Strang Clinics. She never did take her vacation. "I decided then and there that this was perhaps the most important thing that had happened to me in my whole life."

May worked at the Strang Clinics for twenty-nine years, until she retired at age seventy-eight. She examined patients and closely questioned them about their personal and family medical histories. She then used the combined information to discover any existing cancer before it could spread.

Through all those years at the clinic, May continued her family medical practice in Harlem. Her work at the Strang Clinics and her training in public health made her better able to help the poor people whose welfare had always been her first concern. She often took time to visit other neighborhoods where she taught residents to recognize the signs of cancer, so they could get early treatment.

May loved her work and had earned the respect and affection of her colleagues, patients, and neighbors. A career that had once seemed so unlikely was now at its height.

42

CHAPTER 9

The Next Step

May lived in Harlem for the rest of her life. Although she had to retire from the Strang Clinics, she stayed busy with her private practice and her work with New York City's poor children until she was over eighty.

Having had a devoted mother like Lulu and supporters like Dr. Jean Broadhurst and Dr. Elise Strang L'Espérance, May wanted to help other young women who were struggling to succeed. Among them, Dr. Pauli Murray, the first African-American woman ordained an Episcopalian priest, remembered May as a kind, gentle person who took the time to get to know her. When Pauli was a college student, she was in constant danger of malnutrition, like so many other poor New Yorkers. May not only treated her for free, but as Dr. Murray recalled, "She literally pulled me through college."

In 1975, May helped start a society to help African-American women in medical school and to honor their achievements. Two years later, May and five others received awards from the society for "devoted services to their communities for more than fifty years."

Both her college and medical school gave special recognition to May. Calling her a "brave warrior in the fight against sickness, poverty, and injustice," Columbia University awarded her an honorary

doctor of science degree, and Teachers College gave her a Distinguished Alumnus Award. A year later, New York University presented her with a doctor of science degree for her long life of service to Harlem and important work in early cancer detection.

And in 1960, students at a New York City junior high school named her "Our Lady of the Year," presenting her with an award praising "your dedication as a physician; your determination to conquer cancer through research and lectures to the public; your devotion to the welfare of others regardless of race, creed or color."

But despite all the recognition and her advancing age, May kept right on going. On the morning of her eighty-second birthday, she was busy at a health fair in a Harlem church basement checking women for signs of breast cancer. As she had in the past, she adapted the equipment at hand, in this case using a piano bench as an examination table.

May's involvement with young people extended beyond the day-care centers where she had worked for so many years. One of her god-children asked her to become the medical consultant for an organization that sponsored Africans studying in the United States. Though May was eighty-two years old, she began work the next day!

It had been sixty years since May had made her decision to study science, but she always made music a part of her life. Both patients and friends remembered her love of singing and playing the piano. Imagine a doctor who not only comes to your house when you are sick, but who ends her visit with a musical performance!

In December 1980, May collapsed while attending a Columbia University reception in honor of a friend. She died later that evening, after a life of challenge and triumph. Many times throughout May's long life, it would have been helpful to hide her race. But, like her father, she was proud of it. She made it clear that people had to accept her for what she was. "I do what I think is right in my own way," she said. "I can go on without you and I won't make any attempt to win you."

Even though people's opinions weren't very important to May, their actions were. "Become involved with the problems of your Nation, your State, your City, and especially your immediate neighborhood," she wrote. "Help those with problems—help them to take the next step UPWARDS."

INDEX/GLOSSARY

FURTHER READING

To find out more about May Chinn, women in medicine, or important African-Americans, check your local bookstore or ask your librarian. Here are a few books to get you started:

Send us a Lady Physician: Women Doctors in America, 1835-1920
edited by Ruth J. Abram
(New York: W. W. Norton, 1985). The early history of American women in medicine.

Ben Carson by Ben Carson
(Grand Rapids, MI: Zondervan, 1992). The author describes how he went from a troubled inner-city boy to a successful doctor.

This Was Harlem: A Cultural Portrait, 1900-1950
by Jervis Anderson
(New York: Farrar Straus Giroux). An excellent history of Harlem and the people who made it great in the early twentieth century. (Written for adults.)

Acknowledgements:

"A Day to Remember," by Nadine Brozan.
Copyright 1979/1980 The New York Times Company. Reprinted by permission.

The Black Women Oral History Project, v. 2
(Westport, Connecticut: Meckler/K. G. Saur, 1990).

May Edward Chinn Papers
Manuscripts, Archives and Rare Books Division, Schomburg Center for Research in Black Culture; The New York Public Library; Astor, Lenox and Tilden Foundations

"A Healing Hand in Harlem," by George Davis,
The New York Times, April 22, 1979.

The authors wish to thank Professor George Davis, without whose input and generosity this book would have been impossible.

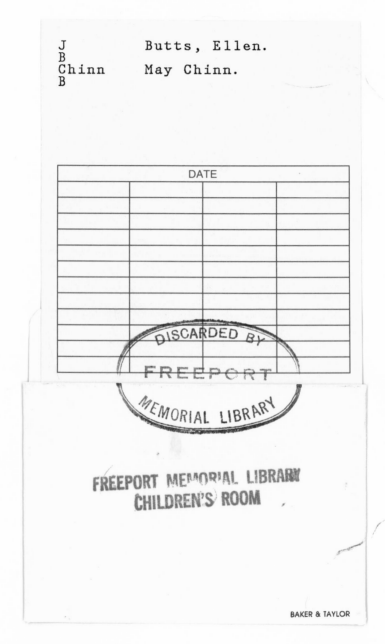

J
B   Butts, Ellen.
Chinn   May Chinn.
B

BAKER & TAYLOR